Time Management

Proven Methods For Increasing Your Productivity And Time Management Strategies

(Secrets Of Time Management And Productivity)

Cristiano Pimentel

TABLE OF CONTENT

Introduction 1
Chapter 1: Successful Time Management 3
Chapter 2: Restoring Balance 7
Chapter 1: Business And Composition 9
Chapter 3: Individuals And Society 11
Chapter 4: Changing Your Email Routines 13
Chapter 5: Nine Frequent Errors In Time Administration 19
Chapter 6: Methods For Establishing Objectives Using Effective Time Management 25
Chapter 7: Time-Dependent Opportunities 31
Chapter 8: The Significance Of Time Administration 36
Chapter 9: Destruction Of Productivity Cockroaches 43
Chapter 10: Time Management Strategies To Enhance Your Writing 46
Chapter 12: Leadership Requires Effective Time Management 66
Chapter 13: Effective Work 73

Chapter 14: Eliminating The Propensity For Procrastination..81

Chapter 15: Think About Your Mission And Objective Think About The Big Picture..............92

Chapter 16: Top Time Management Techniques 96

Chapter 17: Why Does It Operate? 113

Chapter 18: Time Management Versus Efficiency.. 123

Chapter 19: Advice On Time Management That Improves Productivity. 125

Chapter 20: Individualized Time Management For All 129

Chapter 21: Advantages Of Time Management 143

Introduction

For optimal health and personal effectiveness, time management is indispensable. How well you manage your time and life has a significant impact on your inner peace, harmony, and mental health. The perception that time is passing inexorably is the primary source of worry, anxiety, and melancholy.

The more efficiently you plan and manage the significant events in your life, the better you will feel in the present, have more energy, sleep better, and complete more tasks.

By implementing the ideas and techniques discussed in this book, you may be able to increase your daily output by two hours or even double it.

As long as you follow the instructions in this book, these strategies will be just as effective for you as they have been for thousands of executives in a variety of industries.

Chapter 1: Successful Time Management

Your ability to organise your days so that you can complete your duties with less effort and make the most of the time you have available is a crucial aspect of effective time management, which refers to the effective use of your time.

When we are unable to effectively manage our time, the following behaviours are more likely to occur:

Not meeting project deadlines
Produce subpar work Disrupt the healthy balance between our professional and personal lives
Feel more stressed
Ruin our reputation in the professional community.

Let's quickly review the benefits of effective time management so you can gain a better understanding of the topic.

The Advantages of Efficient Time Management

Learning how to effectively manage your time is essential because doing so has numerous positive effects on your daily work activities and your life in general.

Effective time management allows you to achieve your objectives more quickly. When you realise the importance of time management, you gain the motivation to get up from your couch and begin working toward your goals.

You are closer to achieving your goals as a direct result of the effort you have expended and your newly discovered motivation.

Time management allows you to accomplish more in less time: When you effectively manage your time, you not only complete more tasks, but you also have more free time to devote to activities that bring you genuine joy.

The creation of a to-do list, the allocation of a specific amount of time to each item on that list, and the scheduling of that time in your calendar are all components of effective time management.

Effective time management frees up more time for fun activities and makes you feel more energised.

If you can effectively manage your time, you will enjoy the sense of accomplishment that comes with crossing items off your to-do list. The more effort you put into time management, the more confident you will feel that you can accomplish everything on your to-do list. When you realise that you are capable of meeting the standards you have set for yourself, you will develop a greater sense of self-confidence in your abilities.

When you have good time management, you do not need to worry about missing deadlines or forgetting responsibilities. This is because you have already scheduled your time to prevent such errors from occurring. As a result, you will feel less anxious about the amount of work you must complete and more confident about the outcomes.

Effective time management enables you to make positive changes in your life: You can be as productive as a sloth on a duvet day by practising effective time management so that you spend less time being as busy as a bee but still get as much done.You will be able to prioritise the things that are most important to you and organise your time in a way that will allow you to attend your daughter's recital.

Chapter 2: Restoring Balance

It is essential to remember that you are only human, so you must prioritise your own needs. You should schedule time for activities such as socialising with friends, dining out with family, exercising, or simply taking a break from work. When your body and mind are in peak condition, your overall happiness and wellbeing will increase because you will be more stimulated and perform better at work.

It can be very stressful for business owners, especially when the economy is uncertain. To thrive and survive in the work-from-home industry, it may seem reasonable to work longer hours and exert more effort, but doing so will only make matters worse as you become exhausted.

After a long day of making business decisions and attending multiple virtual meetings, happiness and leisure are essential. Balance is the key to both personal and professional happiness and success. Work and play are not necessarily inversely proportional.

Chapter 1: Business And Composition

Having a strong sense of general well-being is the result of achieving balance, which is essential for both personal and professional success. Developing your self-assurance and self-awareness will allow you to achieve the inner balance in your work and personal life that you so desire.

Body, emotion, spirit, and mind are the four primary realms of consciousness. Once you have achieved balance in each of these areas, you will be able to maintain the sense of self-determination required to tackle both professional and personal issues.

Understanding how to maximise profit will contribute to your business success. You are occupied, engaged in enjoyable work, and fostering a positive outlook among all parties.

Combining business and balance has far more potent effects than you could ever imagine. You will enjoy working, others will enjoy working with you, and the task at hand will be successfully completed. Your online advertising company will develop into a market powerhouse.

Chapter 3: Individuals And Society

As a business owner, you have a responsibility to the people, the environment, and the community. Understanding that a company's success requires a mission that transcends the bottom line will help you achieve professional balance.

Numerous businesses in the modern business sector pay insufficient attention to the community in which they operate. These businesses disregard the concerns of their employees, society, and the environment because they believe investors should be their top priority.

Consider carefully which of the issues that are important to you will be supported by your home company. Then, develop a variety of ways for your company to donate. When your organisation has goals and strikes a balance between business, employees, and the community, you will begin to see the effects through profitable expansion.

Chapter 4: Changing Your Email Routines

A ritual raises awareness of something distinctive, which elicits a response. Outsiders and the actor may be unaware of its significance, but a memory, feeling of understanding, or connection lies beneath the action.

A ritual is a presentation consisting of physical motions, objects, and spoken words. While ritual may appear to be simple, the studies claim that it can push individual and organisational behaviour change when done correctly. Creating a ritual around an action may help you reinterpret your experiences and appeal to a larger narrative if you wish to alter your daily activities and ways of thinking.

However, repetition and changing circumstances can diminish the once-magical effect of a ritual over time. Start considering your ritual's function in your daily life if it has lost all meaning and has become a regular part of your routine.

Time is our most valuable resource, but we waste much of it on activities that aren't beneficial, often without even realising it. We have a gazillion tabs loaded with design ideas, YouTube video lessons, Basecamp, etc. open on our desktops. Our to-do list seems to go on forever.

A study indicates that the average person loses 31 hours per year to ineffective meetings. We spend approximately 14 hours per week reading, composing, and responding to email. That leaves around half of your workday to be spent working.

While we are being pulled in more directions than ever before, the internet, clients, and employers are not the only factors preventing us from making the most of our time. We are, in many circumstances, the ones to blame for our loss of work.

This is influenced in part by our thirst for knowledge. Neurotransmitters in the human brain view information as a reward, according to scientific research. This makes evolutionary sense because having access to the right information, such as the locations of food sources, enables us to make better decisions and increases our chances of survival, but it also suggests that we are particularly drawn to distractions that are unrelated to our primary objectives.

Because most of us are happier and more successful when we're busy, we've developed a certain fascination with helpful hints and shortcuts. How can we produce more with fewer resources? What is the key to being productive? No such thing as a secret exists. Many obstacles to efficiency are surmountable with moderate effort.

Routines help us maintain a sense of stability, but they do not always aid in coping with life. While you may spend the very first period of the day composing before your initial consultations, your brain often does not permit such a clear separation between activities.

Here, rituals come into play. Both rituals and routines are recurring activities. However, they have deeper significance than merely a series of events. Consider religious rituals and family traditions. These rituals signify an important change or event that should be noted.

Even during the day, rituals can help guide you and eliminate concentration fatigue during crucial times.

Consider holding a face-to-face meeting rather than creating a document. The mental assumptions of the two individuals differ significantly. We also require the ability to detach from our speech and focus on the person in front of us.

Rituals are quite private. You may take a brief walk, grab a cup of coffee, or put away your computer. Less important than the activity itself is what it signifies to you: that you have completed one portion of your day and are prepared for the next.

Chapter 5: Nine Frequent Errors In Time Administration

Have you ever agreed to a deadline, only to discover that the project required twice as much work as anticipated? Everyone is susceptible to improper planning, which prevents us from making better use of time management. Poor objective-setting practises are also associated with improper planning.

To avoid this error, ensure you have all the information before agreeing to a task. Assess your ability to complete the task in the allotted time with realism. You must figure out how to handle this challenging time management issue by compromising your priorities.

Rapidly and emphatically commit an error. Make sense of the error and adjust the new due date for the project.

There's a lot to be said for the opportunities we open ourselves up to by saying "YES." However, overcommitting ourselves by saying "YES" to too many things can lead to a difficult situation. Employees with a high level of intrinsic motivation frequently take on additional responsibilities and can become exhausted as a result. When we have juggled too many balls, we will stop.

inevitably lose track of some, which could bring down the entire act.

The best way to handle this situation is to be aware of your own limitations and understand that they may change at any time based on the activities you have on your plate or even your own health. Directors should be aware of employees who take on too much, so they can offer assistance or attempt to assume leadership if a worker is overextended.

Numerous employees are becoming more exhausted than ever before. A negative or agitated disposition at the start of the day can become exponentially more regrettable as the day's challenges unfold. When we are emotionally charged, our minds are less able to focus on the task at hand. A decade of research from Harvard Business Review confirms that a negative attitude can have a direct impact on aspects such as financial performance and absenteeism.

To avoid making this error, take breaks throughout the day. The more overwhelmed and emotional you become as the day progresses, the less efficient and productive you will become with your work. Utilize this opportunity to reflect, and get

Get some fresh air, cuddle with your pets or children, or do anything else that will distract you from your work.

Supervisors can aid in promoting employees' health in a variety of ways, including checking in with each employee and promoting the organization's medical benefits.

Decades of research have repeatedly demonstrated that performing multiple tasks simultaneously is not a productive use of time. By dividing our attention, tasks take longer, we lose concentration, and we make more mistakes than if we focused on one thing at a time.

The most efficient method is to concentrate on a single project while simultaneously eliminating distractions. This should prevent you from multitasking. According to the perspective of a task, implementing computer-based intelligence arrangements could help reduce employee workload, thereby reducing the need to perform multiple tasks.

When projects require complex networks of individuals, each responsible for different interlocking components, coordination can break down. Employees will be forced to waste time if the person or group ahead of them has not completed their task. Sequential construction systems must function effectively, which necessitates having the proper personnel for each task phase.

Keep project teams simple and streamlined. Avoid assigning portions of a task to different individuals. This may necessitate a close examination of the company's processes and team management.

Workers who lack the necessary resources to complete assigned tasks will be left with nothing to do and waste their time. This requirement could be for funds, information, or even permission to proceed.

Directors should ensure that employees are able to make decisions and have the necessary resources (funds and information) to move projects forward. Workers should assertively request the resources necessary to complete a task.

Chapter 6: Methods For Establishing Objectives Using Effective Time Management

Step 1: Determine the Available Time

Establishing the amount of time you will devote to your business should be the initial step.

The amount of time you spend at work should reflect the structure of your job and your personal life objectives.

For instance, if you are vying for a promotion, it may be prudent to put in extra time each day to demonstrate your dedication. On the other hand, if you wish to have ample time for extracurricular activities, you can choose to work only the allotted number of hours.

Step 2: Plan Crucial Steps

Next, list the steps you must take to successfully complete the work. These are frequently the standards by which you will be evaluated.

Ensure you have sufficient time to attend to the coaching, monitoring, and personal concerns of your team members if you manage people, for example. Give yourself time to communicate with your employer and other significant people in your life.

The following step involves scheduling your top priorities.

Include high-priority, urgent tasks as well as maintenance tasks that cannot be ignored or outsourced on your to-do list.

Try to schedule them for the times of day when you are most productive; for example, some people are more productive in the morning, when they are most energised and effective, while others are more productive in the afternoon or evening, when they can focus better. Read our article "Is This a Morning Task?" to learn how to determine your optimal times of day.

Step 4: Make emergency preparations

Next, allocate additional time for handling emergencies and unforeseen circumstances. In general, the more unpredictable your task, the more buffer time you will need. Experience will teach you how much leeway to provide. (If you do not plan for this time, crises will still arise, and you will be required to stay late to complete your task.)

Step 5: Schedule Discretionary Time

The remaining time on your schedule is "discretionary time," which can be used to accomplish your priorities and goals. Examine your priority to-do list and personal goals, determine the amount of time required to complete them, and schedule time in your calendar.

Step 6: Evaluate Your Actions

If, by the time you reach step five, you discover that you have little to no free time, you should revisit stages two, three, and four and reevaluate whether all of the tasks you've entered are actually necessary. It is possible that some tasks can be outsourced or completed in a more efficient manner.

Utilizing the leverage you can generate with your time is one of the most important ways to achieve success. You can complete more work by delegating tasks to others, outsourcing essential tasks, and automating as much of your work as possible using technology. This will allow you to accomplish your goals.

If you find that you still have limited free time, you may need to renegotiate your workload or seek assistance. Utilize your recently created schedule as evidence of your numerous obligations. This demonstrates to your manager that you are organised, which can make him or her more receptive to your proposal!

Time management is one of the most important and valuable skills one can possess. If you do not make effective use of your time, there is a very small chance that you will achieve your professional objectives and an even smaller chance that you will achieve your personal objectives.

Chapter 7: Time-Dependent Opportunities

When you begin to practise time management, you will become acutely aware of what you do with your time and where you spend it.

Your current understanding of having more time to do other things leads you to believe that if you choose to do so, you'll automatically lose focus on what's bringing home the bacon, which will negatively impact the bacon. In other words, spending less time at work will not result in a decrease in income.

Assessing the quality of your life, which entails investigating the opportunities you are currently pursuing, is a component of time management. What is the calibre of these possibilities? In this context, time management is the ability to concentrate on opportunities that will bring you joy and satisfaction. Yes, you work, for example, 12 hours per day, and this allows you to drive that nice car or live in that fancy apartment, but why are you reading this book if everything is going so well? You are currently here because something is lacking. You lack complete fulfilment, happiness, and satisfaction despite all your possessions and hard work. Why? Because of the imbalance. Now, suggesting that you quit your job or work fewer hours is not the solution in this situation. Remember that I am not selling a concept that I am unfamiliar with. Everything I preach is founded on my own life experiences. I am well aware that working less will not result in the kind of financial success that you seek.

Consequently, let's take a step back and examine the quality of your opportunities. If you're working yourself to the bone and still feel unhappy and dissatisfied because you don't have enough time to invest in yourself, finding a new job is not necessarily the solution because the goal is not to work harder, but to work smarter. In other words, seek out opportunities that will allow you to put in fewer physical hours while still providing you with greater rewards. Then, we investigate passive income ideas and the like. The concept of passive income is not necessarily focused on this additional income. It's about having something work to your advantage. Here is an opportunity that is putting in the work for you so that you can attend to other matters while still bringing home the desired quality of bacon.

Imagine yourself standing on the peak of a mountain in a remote location, far from the noise and activity of this world. You have a magnificent view of clouds, natural landscapes, and wildlife. When you finally realise how flawlessly and precisely everything is arranged, you'll be overcome by a sense of calm.

There will always be things in your environment that can easily disturb your peace. However, seeking wholeness also involves finding peace. Peace does not mean the absence of something, despite the fact that many may believe that it will be achieved when all problems are resolved. Instead, it means being in the presence of an opportunity that will silence all distractions and bring you to a place of genuine appreciation, where you can recognise how perfectly and precisely everything is arranged.

Constantly seek out moments of gratitude so that you can temporarily escape the stresses and noises of life. This will keep you motivated and content with phases and stages that you will embrace well enough to prevent you from returning to a state of desperation. When you begin to feel this way, your subconscious mind will transport you back to a state of disadvantage, and you'll find yourself back in the rat race.

Freedom is the feeling of being able to do whatever you want, whenever you want. In an ideal world, we would all like to do no work and live as if we practically reside in the office; however, valuing your time means that you want to maximise your free time. In other words, you desire to fill your leisure time with significance.

Chapter 8: The Significance Of Time Administration

For business owners, time is an extremely valuable resource that cannot be stored or saved for later use. Everyone has the same amount of time available to them, but entrepreneurs must understand how to effectively manage their time.

Even if you are unaware of it, time management influences every aspect of your life. It allows you to concentrate on more important tasks, resulting in a significant productivity boost. Over time, increased productivity will yield significant benefits in both your professional and personal lives.

Many individuals believe there is not enough time in their lives to accomplish all of their objectives. They frequently attribute their growing stress, deteriorating relationships, poor finances, and lack of physical fitness to a lack of time. However, if you have excellent time management skills, you can accomplish all of your goals.

Time management can assist you in determining your priorities and making deliberate choices, allowing you to devote more of your time to tasks that will benefit your organisation. Effective time management may also help you achieve your goals more quickly. Time management also allows you to complete more tasks in less time and with less stress and effort.

The Advantages of Time Administration

Time management will result in your becoming more prompt and disciplined. It only forces you to work when necessary. In order to maximise your available time, you must create a to-do list or a task plan. In order to effectively manage your time, you must create a list of activities and tasks that you must complete each day. In addition to specific due dates, you must also indicate the level of urgency for each task on your list. Your task plan, also known as a to-do list, can assist you in maintaining order.

You'll have a stronger sense of direction when it comes to accomplishing your task. It can help you determine how to structure your day so that you work more efficiently and accomplish more in less time.

Being able to manage your time effectively will also help you become more organised. It can demonstrate how to better organise your workspace so that you can quickly locate documents, folders, and files. You can also benefit from your improved time management skills if you employ effective time management techniques.

A time management strategy can also help you achieve your goals and objectives in the shortest amount of time possible. If you have effective time management skills, you may reach your objectives early and finish your work on schedule.

Effective time management can significantly increase your productivity and aid you in achieving your goals without requiring you to work longer hours.

What Effects Can Poor Time Management Have on Your Business?

Ineffective time management in your business can result in a variety of problems and unfavourable outcomes. If you lack effective time management skills, you may experience missed deadlines, subpar work, high stress, inefficient workflow, and other problems.

If you are unable to effectively manage your time, completing your work on time will become increasingly difficult, and you will be perceived as ineffective and unreliable. Your clients, customers, and coworkers will lose faith in your business management abilities. Your reputation will be tarnished by missing deadlines and being late, which will have an effect on your personal life and well-being. If you want to be a successful entrepreneur who accomplishes more in less time, you must learn how to master your time and improve your time management skills.

Chapter 9: Destruction Of Productivity Cockroaches

Examine your day and make note of the time-wasters, such as social media and email, on which you regularly spend ten to twenty minutes. In the world of productivity, these small time-wasters are known as "cockroaches." These activities contribute nothing to your goal attainment.

Give yourself five minutes instead of 20 to 30 minutes to read through your email in the morning. This applies to each of the listed time-filling jobs. Do not focus on these tasks until you have completed your daily to-do list. After you've completed all of your tasks, you can devote as much time as you like to social networking, email reading, and newspaper reading. These are the types of errands in which only 10% of what you accomplish is significant, while the remaining 90% is completely inconsequential; resolving to avoid them until your essential work is completed motivates you to prioritise your efforts.

Utilize the Pomodoro Method.

In the early 1990s, Francesco Cirillo created the Pomodoro Method, which can help you overcome distractions, hyperfocus, and complete tasks in short bursts while taking frequent breaks. This productivity and time management strategy is based on a simple principle: when faced with a series of chores or a large activity, divide it into short, timed intervals with brief breaks in between. This style of work helps you meet deadlines by training your brain to concentrate for brief intervals. The Pomodoro Method is one of the simplest productivity techniques you can employ throughout the day. You will only need a stopwatch. Set a timer for twenty-five minutes and select an item from your to-do list. Work on the assigned task until the timer goes off, then place a checkmark on a sheet of paper. Take a five-minute break, then reset your timer for another quarter-hour and return to your project. Take a longer break ranging from 15 to 30 minutes for every four Pomodoros or checks on your paper. You'll find that if you work in 25-minute intervals with brief breaks in between, you can accomplish a great deal while still taking the necessary breaks to relax and reenergize your mind. If you become distracted for any reason during your 25-minute session, you must either end the Pomodoro or postpone the distraction until the Pomodoro is complete.

Chapter 10: Time Management Strategies To Enhance Your Writing

Daily writing is the most essential activity we perform (at least in the office). But to write well, you must maximise your writing time. Time management allows you to write faster and with greater concentration. Good time management can also help you reduce stress and find time for non-writing tasks.

How Do You Get Better at Time Management?

As I discussed in our post about writer's block, editing is the key to good writing. But how do you find the time to edit multiple draughts when you must also attend meetings, manage other projects, and attend to your own needs? Free up some time and review the following strategies.

Electronic and human interruptions can disrupt your thought process, so avoid them as much as possible. It is natural to want to stay in touch, but you must find peace to write.

Start by turning off your email and phone alerts. This constant stream of alerts is a distraction to writing. Scientists have demonstrated that multitasking hinders productivity and the creative process. Therefore, when writing, keep your smartphone and laptop far away (or better yet, disable notifications).

Even though interacting with people is enjoyable, it can also be distracting, so schedule time when you will close your office door and focus on your work. Simply inform your team when you are prepared to answer their questions. You can also use headphones to block noise and reduce interruptions in a noisy office. Even if you are not listening to music, putting on headphones sends a clear "Do Not Disturb" signal to your coworkers.

Set Clear Objectives: Set objectives to help you manage your time more effectively. Having specific goals in mind can help you stay on track and achieve your objectives; this is true for both the written work product and the time spent writing it.

Start your project by listing its objectives. If we list our objectives prior to writing, we will not forget anything significant. In addition, organising our ideas beforehand helps us determine the optimal way to implement them. Your list may evolve into an outline, which will assist you in organising the specifics of your paper, presentation, study, or document. An outline anchors your main topic and supporting details, thereby improving the flow of your content.

Create a writing schedule in order to manage your time. Even if you aren't working in an office, it helps to establish a regular schedule. For instance, you can write daily from 7:00 a.m. to 11:00 a.m. Do not challenge yourself to the point of discouragement. Instead, set daily, attainable objectives. A manageable daily schedule will assist in reinforcing your writing routine.

Prioritize Difficult Tasks: Have you ever worked on low-priority, simple tasks to avoid difficult ones? Don't deceive yourself with this illusion of productivity; your writing assignment remains unfinished. The best way to approach this situation is head-on.

When writers give priority to their most difficult tasks, they "eat the frog." What does this entail? The author of the best-selling book Eat That Frog, Brian Tracy, suggests that if someone's job is to eat a frog, they should do so first thing in the morning. And if it is their job to consume two frogs, they should begin with the larger one. This sage advice also applies to writing, so prioritise and begin with the most challenging tasks.

I wrote four draughts of this piece before I felt comfortable sending it to my editor, and he typically writes eight or ten draughts before he is satisfied with his own work. Remember that nobody is perfect on the first try.

My strategy is to compose the initial draught as I would say it aloud. I imagine myself explaining it to a friend and record what I hear myself saying. This becomes my initial draught, after which the writing becomes easier. I set it aside in order to attend a meeting, respond to an email, and refill my water bottle.

When I return to my previous draught, I search for awkward phrases and inconsistencies in style. After that, I run it through WordRake before beginning my final round of revisions, during which I focus on avoiding patterns I am aware I should avoid, such as repetitive topic sentences. Then, I perform a final check for typos and homonyms to ensure the document is cohesive and error-free.

Writing does not have to be an all-day endeavour to be beneficial; you can work in shorter spurts. Whenever we have fifteen minutes, or even five, we can frequently revise another draught. Even a handful of these brief writing sessions can help you refine your work and view it with new eyes.

Numerous individuals refer to this method as the Pomodoro technique. It is an effective time management strategy that teaches you how to work in 25-minute intervals with maximum concentration. If you have limited free time, this is a fantastic way to stay focused and productive.

Enhance Your Writing by Improving Your Time Management Abilities Every writer should be able to manage their time effectively, particularly when meeting deadlines. However, even the best-laid plans may fail. Try WordRake when you need an instantaneous edit. The only clear and concise email editor for professionals is WordRake. Microsoft Word and Outlook are supported. WordRake is free to try for seven days.

Chapter 11: Comprehension Of Distractions And Procrastination

I've observed that over the years, more and more people have admitted that procrastination is a problem for them. Negatively affecting not only our never-ending to-do list, but also our sense of self-worth and self-esteem, is delaying chores and failing to accomplish what we intended. We lose faith in ourselves and our ability to advocate for ourselves.

I believe that what the majority of people incorrectly refer to as procrastination is actually a problem with distraction or, worse, a dopamine addiction. Dopamine-releasing applications are practically at our fingertips, and weapons of mass distraction are all around us in this new era.

What function does dopamine play?

The neurotransmitter known as dopamine is associated with pleasure, which is the feeling you get when you buy something new, eat chocolate cake, or open Instagram. This substance is dopamine, which also plays an important role in impulsivity, motivation, and procrastination. Because we live in a culture filled with dopamine-inducing activities, media messages of "do what makes you happy," and hedonistic messages about purchasing the newest gadget or automobile, we are also becoming less adept at tolerating irritation and persevering when we feel disengaged or bored.

When we are working at our desks or studying for an exam and the slightest hint of boredom appears, our brain begins to seek dopamine release. Do you recall your last conversation with your child or a coworker? Did you glance at your phone while they were speaking? Are you curious about who posts on Instagram? You had a dopamine craving at the time.

Former Facebook vice president for user growth Chamath Palihapitiya stated publicly that he felt "a significant degree of remorse" for his role in the creation of dopamine-addicted platforms. We have created dopamine-driven, short-term feedback loops that are detrimental to civilization.

Social media platforms such as Facebook, Snapchat, TikTok, and Instagram use the same brain circuitry as other activities to increase "engagement," which leads to addiction. And in real life, activities such as reading books, completing assignments, and engaging in lengthy discussions do not provide the same steady flow of dopamine; rather, you must endure periods of boredom and frustration.

Dopamine, distraction, or delay of gratification?

Examine your next week's schedule and resolve to complete some challenging tasks. When scheduling these activities into your schedule, be mindful of your time and energy. For example, I will work on this assignment from 2:00 to 4:00 p.m. on Monday. Tuesday at three o'clock I will call my Client. Ensure that the duties align with your career and personal goals.

If you did not complete the assigned tasks, evaluate your performance daily by asking yourself the following questions. How did I feel as I prepared to begin the assigned work? (Are you anxious? worn down? Bored?

Unmotivated?) What did I do instead of beginning? (For example, sleep, watch Netflix, call a friend, browse social media, or work on a different project). How long have I been off the path?

Having the answers to these questions will allow you to identify potential obstacles to achieving your goal. If you were seeking dopamine, you may want to spend less time on social networking sites and more time on Netflix or YouTube. These may be used as a reward for completing chores, but be sure to set a time limit on how long each reward can be utilised. If you are delaying the start or completion of a project, it may be beneficial to determine why you are delaying. It is most likely a result of your inability to manage your time and/or emotions.

We are too quick to label ourselves as procrastinators because we have not considered all the factors that may be preventing us from achieving our objectives. However, we won't be able to effectively address the problem until we determine the underlying cause of our lack of discipline. Spend some time understanding your social media usage patterns and the things that cause you to become distracted or procrastinate.

I only have my laptop, water bottle, and noise-canceling earbuds in front of me when I'm working on a project. I also disable all alerts on my phone, laptop, and computer, leaving only the tab I'm currently using open. Here is how I configure hyperfocus. This is my most productive mode. This allows me to work intensively and uninterruptedly.

Do you know the reason for its effectiveness?

Because I have nothing else on which to focus my thoughts. During these intense work hours, anything novel or enjoyable is removed from my environment. In other words, writing is the sole remaining task. As soon as your task becomes the most stimulating activity for your brain, you'll devote all of your mental resources to it (since there is nothing else to do). The era of delay is over!

Procrastination Is Easily Accessible

As can be seen, distractions foster procrastination. It is quite challenging to resist the allure of new and intellectually stimulating diversions when they are readily available, such as funny cat videos on YouTube, Instagram browsing, checking email every 7 seconds, and monitoring Medium metrics.

The allure of these diversions stems from the fact that they are frequently more pleasurable and intriguing than the subject we should be focusing on. A quick glance at your email or the most recent Instagram photos could send you into an online vortex, costing you 20 minutes that could have and should have been spent productively. You can observe how much focus and productivity you lose by repeatedly doing this throughout the day.

Even worse, it frequently takes us 25 minutes to regain our full concentration on the task at hand after being interrupted (this is something called attention residue, which implies that some of your attention is left behind on the previous task or distraction that you were involved with). When you consider that, on average, individuals who are working at a computer will take a break every 40 seconds, you can see how bad this is. Most individuals have barely begun to utilise their hyperfocus capability. Not remotely close.

The Conflict between Deferred and Immediate Satisfaction

Humans seek the quickest means to experience the greatest arousal. This explains the immense popularity of fast food, porn, drugs, alcohol, and social media. They provide us with massive dopamine surges that boost our mood without any effort on our part. In essence, we are rewarded for actions that do not contribute to a meaningful, satisfying existence. That's a little off, wouldn't you say?

The majority of our employers do not provide us with these chemicals that produce an immediate feeling of well-being. The majority of our efforts will eventually bear fruit, whether monetarily, spiritually, physically, or in terms of our relationships. In other words, regardless of whether the delay is two hours or two months, our labour brings us delayed satisfaction. The challenge remains that the reward is earned in the future and not immediately, despite the fact that it is frequently far more substantial than any form of instant gratification.

This is precisely why the majority of people procrastinate so much. It explains why they have such a difficult time completing their tasks, advancing effectively, and finishing tasks. You're in trouble when instant gratification is a swipe, click, or bite away.

Prior to focusing on the most essential tasks, we must first deal with potential distractions. The optimal strategy for winning this fight is to never enter the ring. We must create a distraction-free environment that allows us to focus on our tasks for extended periods of time. This permits us to at least double our productivity and cease procrastination.

Seven Steps To A Hyperfocus, Distraction-Free Work Process

I will now describe the seven steps I take to organise distraction-free, hyper-focused work sessions in order to complete my most important tasks as efficiently and effectively as possible. I should note that I only use this method for my most important and crucial projects, not for less important or valuable tasks. You can only devote a limited number of hours per day to intense work, so make the most of the time you have. Utilize your valuable, limited mental resources on the most challenging, consequential tasks that will have the greatest impact on your life or business. I believe it is acceptable to perform less important tasks in a more relaxed manner.

Chapter 12: Leadership Requires Effective Time Management

Good leaders are also effective time managers. What origin? Because they are taking crucial steps to achieve the organization's objectives. You examine the environment, identify things and areas that require modification, and apply the principles to make them functional.

Good time managers are also able to guide and inspire others to discover their own methods for better time management. They lead by example and provide free assistance and information.

As leaders, they are always willing to share methods, tips, and techniques that can help others manage their time, problems, and situations more effectively.

Guide

In an online business, entrepreneurs must work on multiple projects and businesses simultaneously and have a time manager who can efficiently manage them all.

Network operators cannot experience commercial success if they lose customers, run out of time, fail to charge customers for their time, or fail to complete projects.

Her ability to successfully complete a project is one of the key indicators that she is a time-savvy entrepreneur. Will they survive the crisis, and if so, will they do so with purpose? Is slow and fast project management part of the objective, and will they contribute to achieving it?

The effect this has on the work of home-based business owners can have an effect on their future business prospects and reputation as well. Integrated. Do you have a solution for this obstacle?

Time = Management

Effective time management is likely the top priority for the majority of DIY enthusiasts in their pursuit of success. Without efficient time management, their web-based enterprise would fail.

The goal of nearly every home-based entrepreneur who wishes to be successful is the efficient use of time. Effective time management enables business owners to accomplish more, keep customers satisfied, and maintain a well-organized enterprise.

Web entrepreneurs require a specific set of skills, strategies, and tools for effective time management in order to complete specific tasks, projects, and objectives. Without strategic time management, they are essentially wasting their time and unable to achieve crucial business objectives.

Numerous factors make it crucial for the Internet entrepreneur to effectively manage time in their home business:

- They are capable of completing projects on time

If they can effectively complete projects, they can take on more work, hire more employees, and better serve their clients by meeting deadlines.

- They are more capable of producing quality work.

When more time and attention are devoted to the details of a task, higher-quality work is produced. Detail-oriented care and thoroughness may be the only way to ensure quality work.

- They may obtain more work if they can meet deadlines.

As a home-based entrepreneur, meeting customer deadlines is tantamount to a work guarantee! Virtually everything on the Internet is time-sensitive, so meeting deadlines demonstrates your responsibility and dedication to the task at hand. Once an entrepreneur has mastered the art of time management, examining the core details of his business will yield a substantial return on investment. The more you can accomplish over a period of time, the less time it will take to complete the task, but the more money you will need to do so.

The return on investment (time spent planning) is substantial.

- Satisfied

When an online entrepreneur completes a task, there is a general sense of satisfaction and achievement. A sense of accomplishment is motivating and provides the inspiration necessary to target new customers or do more business with existing ones.

These factors frequently motivate home-based workers to devise their own methods for better time management and increased productivity. Typically, it is the small details of running a business (such as time management) that aid an entrepreneur in navigating his or her business.

Still, when entrepreneurs attempt to accomplish a great deal over the course of a business relationship, it is not always easy and pleasant times. When they are responsible for every aspect of the business, failure and frustration are always possible due to a lack of planning and organisation.

What occurs when time management fails or desired results are not achieved? Do all network entrepreneurs face difficulties with time management?

Occasionally, a DIY enthusiast discovers that a system or procedure is ineffective. No matter what they do, they are unable to maintain concentration and complete their tasks and objectives. They discover that they have fundamentally mismanaged their time and are unable to accomplish small or large objectives.

Who is the offender? Poor time management.

Chapter 13: Effective Work

Five Strategies for Achieving More in Less Time

Summary. You have more work than you can complete in the allotted time using your current methods. Clearly, you have established your priorities. You have an approach. You have passed it on to someone else. You have attempted to zero in on something. Improving your productivity so that you can complete the same amount of work in less time is the next big thing. Here...more

Post on Twitter and online, and Save, Duplicate, and Distribute

You will never complete all of your tasks if you continue your current pace. Your priorities are set. What you've done is deliberate. What you've done is delegate.

You have tried to concentrate. Productivity's next frontier is efficiency gains, which allow you to do the same or similar work in less time.

The most effective strategies for you depend on your unique personality and circumstances. As a time management coach, I assist individuals like you who need to complete more in less time, and I can tell you from experience that if you implement even one of the following five techniques, you will reclaim hours per week.

Prior to undertaking any substantial project, it is essential to discuss expectations with all relevant parties. It is possible that a PowerPoint presentation is not required. Perhaps they need a job where they can earn an A+, but a B+ will suffice. Perhaps a rough outline is sufficient, but it's more likely that they'll need something more comprehensive.

One of the finance professionals I've coached reported saving several days of time after realising that in certain situations, a simple yes-or-no response suffices. An exhaustive investigation was not always necessary.

The time spent deciding what to do and completing tasks can be reduced by several hours if you first determine what is required and to what extent.

The amount of time saved by reusing and recycling tasks is dependent on the nature of your job. When possible, use copy/paste and editing tools. This could occur in virtually any circumstance in which you are communicating in a very similar manner, including emails, presentations, trainings, proposals, etc.

Establish Sample Documents and Checklists.

A template or checklist can expedite the completion of routine tasks. As an example, I use a yearly tax email template that I send to my accountant and personalise with pertinent financial information at the end of the year. Regarding my monthly financial routine, I use a checklist.

Activities such as creating weekly reports, presentations, and meeting agendas could all benefit from using templates. Checklists can also be useful for weekly planning, one-on-one meetings, and anything else that requires regular completion. If you use a template or a checklist, you can accomplish more in less time because you will not waste time trying to remember what to do or determining what to do next.

Although you could use a more elaborate system to store your templates and checklists, I've found that storing them in a Microsoft Word document is usually adequate.

Commence a Discussion

It may be possible to save time when communicating verbally about completed work. Perhaps your boss has assigned you the task of conducting research. Given the time constraints, it may be more efficient to simply take notes and discuss the results of your research in a one-on-one setting than to compose a formal presentation.

This technique is also useful when attempting to communicate more abstract concepts, such as those involved in the design process. One of my coaching clients discovered that verbalising or sketching out her ideas with an architect was significantly faster than writing them down.

Limiting Working Hours

Lastly, setting a time limit for yourself and sticking to it is one way to complete a task quickly and effectively in less time. If you tend to spend too much time conducting research, for example, you might tell yourself you must stop after an hour or two. Alternatively, if you have trouble coming up with an introduction, you can decide beforehand how much time you are willing to spend typing something up.

Utilizing time constraints does not guarantee that tasks will be completed on time. However, this is something that can benefit concentration. And remembering that Parkinson's Law states that "work expands so as to fill the time allotted to it" is useful if you set a time limit for yourself beforehand.

Even if you follow the above suggestions, I cannot guarantee that everything will be completed; we all have limitations. When these methods are utilised, however, more work is completed in less time.

Read up on how to boost your own productivity and related topics. Time and process administration

Chapter 14: Eliminating The Propensity For Procrastination

It is possible to avoid wasting time. The following are five essential considerations to ensure that you can continue to end your foolish stalling habit.

Examine your justifications and the rational stories you tell yourself. By testing your opinion, could you become a "expert disputer" in the future?

Create a daily or weekly plan for the day, and keep track of your progress. Upon completion, mark off those momentary tasks and then reward yourself. Tell the truth about what has not yet been completed.

Move forward and seek assistance. If you are having difficulty completing an assignment, you should make it public.

Consult a mentor, companion, or leader for assistance in establishing your credibility as a responsible individual. By enlisting the aid of others, you can accept responsibility when you feel frustrated.

Attend to business. Choose a task that you truly abhor performing (like setting up interviews). Focus on doing it daily for only 10 minutes. Observe that once you've begun, you can enter your stream state again and again without difficulty.

Adapt to stress, pressure, and unease. You can utilise a variety of techniques to help you manage your stress and anxiety. For example, practise deep breathing or moderate muscle relaxation.

You could keep an actual activity plan that is predictable. Alternatively, you could listen to music, unwind tapes, or find humour in your everyday life.

Begin little. By implementing small changes, you will create opportunities to learn and develop to become your best self. There is nothing you cannot accomplish, and the ability to effect change resides within you.

Conquering procrastination is not a simple feat. Despite this, I am confident that you will be able to implement the desired change with the proper tools, mindset, and emotionally supportive network.

Effective time management is one of the adaptable skills generally desired by managers in the current labour market, regardless of position. Individuals who effectively manage their time are less anxious, produce higher-quality work, and are required to adhere to time constraints. If this association does not work out easily for you, the good news is that it is quite possible to obtain. Utilizing time effectively has long intrigued analysts, who have developed a variety of techniques. Coffee Occupations contains ten tips for more effectively utilising time in the workplace or while seeking employment.

Establish objectives.

Ask yourself which objectives are most important to you at the moment and how they should be achieved. These objectives should be reasonable and measurable. If you're aiming for an executive position in an organisation, begin by dividing this objective into a few substantial activities spread out over time.

For example:

Change CV Registration for Executive Programs

Attend a systems administration event.

Apply to become a board member

Remember to reward yourself once you've accomplished your goals!

2. Make a daily schedule.

You risk forgetting arrangements and missing deadlines if you attempt to remember your schedule. Utilize applications such as Google Schedule, Todoist, or Evernote to manage your checklists. Certain individuals prioritise their tasks using a variety of coded structures or letters. Indeed, make sure your errands are specific and concrete.

Transform your objectives into behaviours.

To cultivate a habit, repeat similar errands consistently, simultaneously, and in the same location. For example, to improve your writing skills, set the goal of reading every night before bed and writing for 30 minutes at noon.

Emphasis on.

Utilize the Eisenhower grid to categorise your tasks according to their urgency and significance.

Immediate completion is required for all serious and weighty tasks.

Significant but non-urgent tasks: determine whether they can be deferred or outsourced.

Relevant and important assignments: complete them or delegate them immediately.

Irrelevant and unimportant tasks: disregard them.

5. Delegate when vital.

You must be able to recognise when you have a substantial amount of work to complete. Master the art of saying "no" and delegate your errands. This may require a substantial amount of modesty, but the end result will be superior.

Calculate the time spent on each of your assignments.

Utilizing a schedule or planner, evaluate how you spend your time throughout the day. You may or may not recognise that your time has been extensively consumed. First, create a schedule broken down by the half hour, from morning until bedtime. Perform this task during a typical week. Document your activities during every half-hour interval. You can then create a schedule based on your decisions.

7. Steer clear of interruptions.

Arrange the deck to your advantage. Focus your energy with the intention of achieving a state of complete concentration. If you really want to, turn off your phone and sign out of your meetings via online entertainment.

8. enjoy frequent reprieves

After working diligently for sixty minutes on a project, take a break to clear your mind.

Understanding Personal development

In the event that we are considering personal development, it is useful to be judicious about where we put our efforts so that we don't waste time on inappropriate things. A few aspects of ourselves are generally inconsistent, whereas a few of our perspectives are incredibly stable. Thus, we are best served by focusing our efforts on the most modifiable aspects of ourselves.

Given that there are businesses out there telling us that we can change any aspect of ourselves, it is typically difficult for us to know precisely what and how to change. Fortunately, a prominent mental specialist, Martin Seligman, provided accurate information about the aspects of ourselves that we can improve (and those that we cannot), as indicated by the research.

Several aspects of personal development include:

Alarm

Sexual difficulties

Temperament

Discouragement

Hopefulness

Despite the fact that there may be other aspects of our ideal selves to develop, this article will focus exclusively on these logically supported areas.

All-Access Pass - Health PLR Content Collection

Chapter 15: Think About Your Mission And Objective Think About The Big Picture

Be specific about the outcomes you desire. What is your desired objective, outcome, or accomplishment? As recommended by Stephen Covey, begin with the end in mind. Where do you wish to be at the end of the day? As you climb the success ladder, ensure that it is resting against the correct structure. Are you attempting to generate a sufficient income that will allow you to feel content and comfortable? Do you work because you enjoy it, or because you feel compelled to accomplish something of great significance? How would your world look if you achieved your highest aspiration? What long-term career and personal objectives do you have? What is your purpose? What effect do you hope to have on the lives of others? If your only motivation for working is to earn enough money to cover your expenses, it will be difficult to develop and maintain a high level of commitment and enthusiasm. To be truly happy and fulfilled, you must be working toward something greater than yourself that impacts the lives or careers of others.

Once you have decided what you wish to accomplish, you must consider how you will do so. Every time you ask and answer these two questions, you will gain valuable insights that will enable you to assess your situation and determine whether you are moving in the right direction. The third question you must ask is, "How is it going?" when you are certain of what you are trying to accomplish and how you are trying to accomplish it. Is what you're doing helping you achieve your goals as quickly and efficiently as possible? Are you satisfied with your rate of advancement? Are you encountering an excessive amount of obstacles and problems along the way? Above all else, verify your assumptions. In the words of Peter Drucker, all failures are caused by false assumptions.

What assumptions do you have regarding your life and work? What conscious assumptions do you hold? What unfounded assumptions do you frequently fail to verify? It is astounding how many hardworking individuals devote long hours to unfounded assumptions they have never questioned.

Reflecting on the How are you doing?

You should also consider the following essential question: Could there be an alternative? The reality is that there is almost always a superior way to achieve a business objective. This alternative strategy may be more effective, faster, less expensive, and easier. A beautiful line states that there is more to life than just increasing its speed. Despite exerting considerable effort, many individuals are on the wrong path. They are unsure of what they are attempting to do or where they wish to go, but they do not wish to consider the possibility that they are mistaken. Asking difficult questions requires deliberate thought, but it can significantly accelerate the rate at which you achieve your vision, mission, and company objectives.

Chapter 16: Top Time Management Techniques

You can choose a course of action by identifying your most time-consuming responsibilities and assessing whether you are prioritising the most important tasks. Knowing how much time is required for routine tasks could help you plan and estimate more accurately for other projects.

You press the alarm button and cover your face with the covers for an additional five minutes as you begin to awaken to annoying noise. You reach for your phone before drifting off to sleep in order to check your emails and social media feeds. You believe that you are prepared for the next day, but then anxiety sets in. Your manager is ungrateful and eager for you to begin working.

The amusing portion is about to begin. You take a tense shower while crying into the soothing water and listening to Blink-182 music. Your day has finally gotten underway. Nevertheless, you discover upon acquisition that your favourite outfit is at the laundromat.

Before leaving the house, you frantically grab a steaming cup of coffee to combat the persistent dizziness caused by your lack of sleep. After the coffee takes effect, you begin to feel normal. You read the headlines to educate yourself because you are exhausted from travel and dislike your clumsy hands. As you are repeatedly told how unjust and dangerous the world is and how it is about to end, your body produces more cortisol. You finally reach your workplace. Despite your desperate need for sleep, you cannot fall asleep. You reluctantly begin working on the growing list of responsibilities. Perhaps lunch will be served shortly. Although this may appear dramatic, you will comprehend the point. Some of us have terrible or terrible awakenings. In addition, we frequently disregard or accept our limited morning circumstances under the guise of "not being coffee drinkers" or "being too busy."

Here is a 15-minute morning routine to assist you in conquering the day.

Offset Your Cell (0 Minutes)

Pick up the phone after completing your morning routine. Emails, communications, and alerts cannot be delayed by more than fifteen minutes. If, like the majority of us, you are dependent on your smartphone, you must exercise caution. If you desire a more favourable pattern later in the day, you should avoid it in the morning.

Consume an Abundance of water (1 Minute)

If you get up every hour throughout the night to drink water, you will be dehydrated upon awakening. Instead of experiencing fatigue, headache, tension, and mood swings due to depletion, provide your cells with the necessary water bath.

Obtain Sunlight (2-5 Minutes)
The sun shines upon you. It provides energy and aids in the regulation of your circadian rhythm, alerting your mind that it is time to rise.

Workout (2-5 Minutes) (2-5 Minutes)
Two to five minutes of exercise in the morning can keep you energised throughout the day. Maximize your productivity by slightly extending your legs and arms.

Buffet, one of the world's most successful businessmen, questions the necessity of these goals. Instead, he attributes his success to abandoning less important objectives in order to concentrate on those that would produce the desired results. With a net worth of over $70 billion and ownership of more than 70 companies through his property investment firm Berkshire Hathaway, Warren Buffett has demonstrated his proficiency in prioritising essential tasks. However, this level of concentration is uncommon. When there are numerous options, the majority of us experience decision anxiety. Fortunately, Buffett has a solution. According to a story told by Buffett's private pilot, Mike Flint, the investor has a straightforward method for determining which projects require his attention. This approach may be used for both short-term and long-term goals, as Flint asked whether professional objectives should be prioritised. Buffett and Flint discussed this activity, and Buffett decided to focus on the five most important objectives he had listed. He said he would work on them when he got the chance, but the other 20 were indeed important to him.

It makes sense that way. Although they were not in the top 5, their choices were not terrible. What was Buffett's response to this claim?

You have got it backward, Mike. Your list of items to attempt to avoid was anything you did not circle. No matter what, until you have finished your top 5, you will never be listening to this material.

Why do we wish to eliminate "good" lifestyle decisions?

Buffett recognised that, despite the existence of "good" options or goals to pursue, everything on the preceding list is only a distraction from the realities of everyday living.

It is comparable to packing your winter coat, boots, and shoes for a weekend getaway to a warm climate. Although being prepared is a great concept, you are hauling unnecessary baggage that is just making you feel worse.

Every action we do and choice we make has a price. Additionally, deciding whether to focus on your major or secondary list saps your excitement and drive. Every activity has a cost. Even activities that seem neutral are not unbiased. They demand time, energy, and space that may be better used on more crucial tasks or better actions. Rather than doing any action, we are typically in a condition of motion. This is what makes Warren Buffett's strategy so effective. Six through twenty-five on your checklist are the issues you care about. They are necessary for you. It is easy to justify giving them your full attention. However, these products are a distraction compared to your top five goals. You had 20 unfinished projects.

Warren Buffett has shown the worth of his counsel. Make a thorough list of your objectives and follow them. Please list your top 25 priorities, and then order them immediately. Then, start concentrating on achieving your top five goals!

It has been over a century since the Ivy Lee Technique first appeared. It is deceptively simple, but since it focuses on setting priorities and deleting pointless and inconsequential activities from your daily schedule, it is still quite useful and relevant today.

The Ivy Lee approach dates back to 1918, when Bethlehem Steel Company chairman Charles Schwab hired Lee, a productivity consultant, to assist him in increasing corporate productivity. The story is that Lee gave Schwab his method for free, and after three months, the chief was so pleased with the results that he sent Lee a check for $25,000 (around $400,000 in today's dollars).

Focusing on a small number of important activities throughout the day results in maximum efficiency and productivity instead of tasking, which divides your attention across multiple projects, leaving you feeling busy and occupied but never doing anything of significance.

Give yourself no more than six essential tasks each day, organise them from much to least important, and focus on and complete them in that order. Once you have completed the primary task, go on to the next one. Note your goals for the next day after the workday. Repeat each day, putting any unfinished tasks at the top of the six-item list for the next day.

The Ivy Lee method dictates that you must focus on one task at a time, moving from the most important to the least important items on the list until you have completed them all. Any remaining tasks must be added to the six-item list for the following day. By planning your day the night before, you can reduce mental fatigue and save energy for the most important tasks. You attempt to wake up knowing exactly what you have been doing all day, rather than spending valuable time and energy in the morning making decisions.

Using the Ivy Lee method, new work is also "eliminated from the friction of commencement." You may be more productive in the morning if you select your most important task the night before. This can prevent confusion and wasted time the following morning.

Add to tomorrow's to-do list everything that was not completed today. Ask yourself if it is necessary to include a task on your to-do list if it consumes enough of your focus for multiple days in a row. Typically, a task that requires many days or weeks to complete is not essential to begin with. After a day, restart from phase one.

Why Does It Operate?

The greatest strength of the Ivy Lee Theory is its clarity. Developing a new routine may be difficult at times. It may take several days to remember and practise every step. This approach is the polar opposite. A few days are all it takes for the treatments to become routine.

2. a sharp focus

Variety has been observed to be useless. Regardless of how proficient you believe you are at multitasking, you are significantly more productive when concentrating on a single task. There are interruptions in the real world. Expecting you to be able to avoid multitasking successfully is ridiculous. The more time you spend focusing only on one thing, the more productive you will be.

3. Shortens the time needed to make a decision.

You select inferior options. The more choices you make daily. This is described by the term "decision fatigue." Using the discussed strategy, you must make all significant decisions the night before. With this strategy, you may spend less time deciding how to proceed and more time carrying out the action.

To determine which activities will work best for you, try out a variety of options. In general, the quantity of tasks must be both challenging and reasonable. You would not want to complete everything in the remaining time. In addition, you do not want to be so overburdened with work that you must delay it until the next day.

The Eisenhower Structure is a simple decision-making technique that can help you determine which tasks are essential, not essential, urgent, and non-urgent. It divides tasks into four columns and identifies those that will be reassigned or eliminated, as well as those that should be prioritised first.

It is also known as the Urgent-Important Matrix, and Stephen Covey popularised it in The Seven Habits of Highly Intelligent People. It was given this name in honour of Dwight Eisenhower, the 34th President of the United States, who was known for his effectiveness and organisation. According to legend, Dwight Eisenhower prioritised his tasks, as only the most important and urgent documents were sent to his desk.

The Eisenhower Matrix separates your to-do list into essential and urgent tasks, allowing you to delegate or ignore the latter. The distinction between urgent and important tasks served as the matrix's foundation.

People often assume that all urgent tasks are of equal importance, despite the fact that this has not always been the case. This misunderstanding can be attributed to our propensity to prioritise urgent problems and challenges.

Four quadrants

Perform Initial quadrant

In quadrant one, or the "do" quadrant, you should place all necessary and important actions. When an item on your to-do list requires immediate attention, has clear repercussions, or affects your long-term objectives, place it in this box.

The Second Quadrant is listed on the agenda.

Any tasks that are necessary but not urgent should be placed in the "schedule" square in the second quadrant. Some tasks that have an impact on your long-term objectives but do not need to be completed immediately can be delayed. You will complete these tasks after completing those in quadrant one.

Third Quadrant Representative

In the "delegate" quadrant, also known as quadrant 3, you should place urgent but unimportant tasks. Even if they must be completed immediately, these tasks are irrelevant to your long-term objectives. Delegating tasks is one of the best ways to reduce your workload and help your team develop new skills.

The Fourth Quadrant ought to be eliminated.

After reviewing your to-do list and assigning items to the first three categories, a few tasks will remain. The remaining positions were surplus to requirements. These irrelevant side distractions hinder your ability to achieve your objectives. The remaining items on your to-do lists should be placed in the "delete" quadrant.

If you've created to-do lists and whittled them down to the bare essentials, but you're still not getting things done, you should consider creating and sticking to a schedule.

For some, a simple to-do list is sufficient for productivity. This is typically the type of person who just wants to get things over with as soon as possible and, as a result, completes their to-do list early so they can go out to dinner or something.

For others, however, a to-do list is simply too vague, and they find themselves constantly postponing tasks because they lack motivation. Oh, procrastination, a whole chapter will be devoted to you.) Thus, a daily schedule is necessary.

A daily schedule is essentially a list of tasks with timestamps. On a schedule, "fold the laundry from 10:00 to 10:30" will appear where "fold the laundry" would appear on a to-do list. Having a specific amount of time attached to a task can motivate you to complete it, because your brain subconsciously recognises that if you don't do it now, you won't have time to do it later.

Therefore, should you utilise a task list or a schedule? To reach a conclusion, you must evaluate the primary pros and cons of each option.

The major advantage of using only a to-do list is that it is very flexible and you can do things at your own pace, so even if your day gets derailed, you can rearrange your to-do list and still complete your tasks. This is also the greatest disadvantage. If you lack commitment and discipline, your to-do list may become a "to-do someday" list. Or, you could continue to postpone tasks until you are forced to stay up all night in order to complete them, which would be equally detrimental.

The primary advantage of a schedule is that it provides structure and gives you a precise idea of not only what you must do throughout the day, but also when you must do it. In this way, it assists you in organising your day to be as productive as possible, as opposed to floundering around unsure of what to do and when. The greatest disadvantage of using a schedule is that it may be too rigid. If something unexpected occurs or you complete a task in excess of the allotted time, it can throw off your entire schedule and increase your stress levels.

The best way to determine which one is best for you is to test out both and determine which one produces superior results. Unfortunately, as with most things, trial and error, which will take time, is the only way to truly grasp both techniques and modify them to your liking. I understand that we all desire immediate results, especially when it comes to being productive, but sometimes we must be patient and allow time and repetition to do their work.

What I can do for you in the interim is provide some scheduling advice.

Scheduling is similar to a to-do list with an additional step, so many of the tips for to-do lists can also be applied to schedules. As you would with a to-do list, you will still need to break down your tasks into small chunks and then prioritise them. Only this time, you'll give yourself a specific amount of time to complete each bite-sized chunk.

Chapter 17: Why Does It Operate?

The greatest strength of the Ivy Lee Theory is its clarity. Developing a new routine may be difficult at times. It may take several days to remember and practise every step. This approach is the polar opposite. A few days are all it takes for the treatments to become routine.

2. a sharp focus

Variety has been observed to be useless. Regardless of how proficient you believe you are at multitasking, you are significantly more productive when concentrating on a single task. The real world contains interruptions. Expecting you to successfully avoid multitasking is ridiculous. The more time you devote to a single task, the more productive you will become.

Reduces the time required to make a choice.

You select inferior options. The more choices you make daily. This is described by the term "decision fatigue." Using the discussed strategy, you must make all significant decisions the night before. With this strategy, you may spend less time deciding how to proceed and more time carrying out the action.

To determine which activities will work best for you, try out a variety of options. In general, the quantity of tasks must be both challenging and reasonable. You would not want to complete everything in the remaining time. In addition, you do not want to be so overburdened with work that you must delay it until the next day.

The Eisenhower Structure is a simple decision-making technique that can help you determine which tasks are essential, not essential, urgent, and non-urgent. It divides tasks into four columns and identifies those that will be reassigned or eliminated, as well as those that should be prioritised first.

It is also known as the Urgent-Important Matrix, and Stephen Covey popularised it in The Seven Habits of Highly Intelligent People. It was named after the 34th President of the United States, Dwight Eisenhower, who was known for his efficiency and organisation. According to legend, Dwight Eisenhower prioritised his tasks, as only the most important and urgent documents were sent to his desk.

The Eisenhower Matrix separates your to-do list into essential and urgent tasks, allowing you to delegate or ignore the latter. The distinction between urgent and important tasks served as the matrix's foundation.

People often assume that all urgent tasks are of equal importance, despite the fact that this has not always been the case. This misunderstanding can be attributed to our propensity to prioritise urgent problems and challenges.

Four quadrants

Perform Initial quadrant

In quadrant one, or the "do" quadrant, you should place all necessary and important actions. When an item on your to-do list requires immediate attention, has clear repercussions, or affects your long-term objectives, place it in this box.

The Second Quadrant is listed on the agenda.

Any tasks that are necessary but not urgent should be placed in the "schedule" square in the second quadrant. Some tasks that have an impact on your long-term objectives but do not need to be completed immediately can be delayed. You will complete these tasks after completing those in quadrant one.

Third Quadrant Representative

In the "delegate" quadrant, also known as quadrant 3, you should place urgent but unimportant tasks. Even if they must be completed immediately, these tasks are irrelevant to your long-term objectives. Delegating tasks is one of the best ways to reduce your workload and help your team develop new skills.

The Fourth Quadrant ought to be eliminated.

After reviewing your to-do list and assigning items to the first three categories, a few tasks will remain. The remaining positions were surplus to requirements. These irrelevant side distractions hinder your ability to achieve your objectives. The remaining items on your to-do lists should be placed in the "delete" quadrant.

If you've created to-do lists and whittled them down to the bare essentials, but you're still not getting things done, you should consider creating and sticking to a schedule.

For some, a simple to-do list is sufficient for productivity. This is typically the type of person who just wants to get things over with as soon as possible and, as a result, completes their to-do list early so they can go out to dinner or something.

For others, however, a to-do list is simply too vague, and they find themselves constantly postponing tasks because they lack motivation. Oh, procrastination, a whole chapter will be devoted to you.) Thus, a daily schedule is necessary.

A daily schedule is essentially a list of tasks with timestamps. On a schedule, "fold the laundry from 10:00 to 10:30" will appear where "fold the laundry" would appear on a to-do list. Having a specific amount of time attached to a task can motivate you to complete it, because your brain subconsciously recognises that if you don't do it now, you won't have time to do it later.

Therefore, should you utilise a task list or a schedule? To reach a conclusion, you must evaluate the primary pros and cons of each option.

The major advantage of using only a to-do list is that it is very flexible and you can do things at your own pace, so even if your day gets derailed, you can rearrange your to-do list and still complete your tasks. This is also the greatest disadvantage. If you lack commitment and discipline, your to-do list may become a "to-do someday" list. Or, you could continue to postpone tasks until you are forced to stay up all night in order to complete them, which would be equally detrimental.

The primary advantage of a schedule is that it provides structure and gives you a precise idea of not only what you must do throughout the day, but also when you must do it. In this way, it assists you in organising your day to be as productive as possible, as opposed to floundering around unsure of what to do and when. The greatest disadvantage of using a schedule is that it may be too rigid. If something unexpected occurs or you complete a task in excess of the allotted time, it can throw off your entire schedule and increase your stress levels.

The best way to determine which one is best for you is to test out both and determine which one produces superior results. Unfortunately, as with most things, trial and error, which will take time, is the only way to truly grasp both techniques and modify them to your liking. I understand that we all desire immediate results, especially when it comes to being productive, but sometimes we must be patient and allow time and repetition to do their work.

What I can do for you in the interim is provide some scheduling advice.

Scheduling is similar to a to-do list with an additional step, so many of the tips for to-do lists can also be applied to schedules. As you would with a to-do list, you will still need to break down your tasks into small chunks and then prioritise them. Only this time, you'll give yourself a specific amount of time to complete each bite-sized chunk.

Chapter 18: Time Management Versus Efficiency.

In general, productivity refers to the number of activities planned within a given time period. If we consider two individuals (let's call them Carl and Carson) and Carl adapts to two similar daily activities while Carson manages only one, Carl will be deemed more valuable. However, does this imply that Carl uses time management techniques to complete tasks? This is subject to discretion. The following are a few examples of how people typically measure productivity:

Time management skills are essential for meeting deadlines and being the most valuable employee in your organisation.

In any case, they are not the only things you desire for that purpose. Experience, method, strategies, and both hard and soft skills contribute to your prosperity. Time management is a distinct discipline in response to questions about monitoring productivity, establishing boundaries, and efficiently organising work processes. In this way, productivity and the use of time management are interconnected despite existing independently. We are currently discussing highly effective productivity tips, so let's discuss time management hacks that will increase your productivity.

Chapter 19: Advice On Time Management That Improves Productivity.

1. Track Time Usage

Regardless of how much time you devote to exercises, if you are attempting to achieve aggressive objectives, you should focus on achieving results quickly. Evaluating how you spend your typical business days will help you eliminate time-wasters and procrastinators. Use a paper journal or an application to keep tabs on everything.

Create a period journal with 15-minute intervals. Record all of your daily activities. Examining your schedule at the end of the day will reveal interruptions and demonstrate whether or not the day's objectives were accomplished. Additionally, you will discover your most productive time of day. The examination will reveal how much time you devote to various types of tasks. Perhaps the idea of attending the subsequent online course will ring a bell. Effectiveness is founded on capabilities and experience.

Plan and organise.
The method of tracking what you do during the day can be improved by scheduling your upcoming extended periods of time. Ensure you will have sufficient energy for everything by prioritising the most important and laborious tasks. Set reminders or updates for when you need to switch between tasks. Here are some scheduling tips:

Try to employ a single method for monitoring your activities. If it is a flexible application, add new tasks directly there; do not keep track of them separately in a notepad or on a sticky note. This will only lead to disorganisation, and important activities may become buried under a mountain of paper!

If you use both electronic and paper organisers, you should spend two or three minutes per day matching them.

Using mobile applications is more efficient because you always have your cell phone on you, whereas carrying a paper notepad around could be awkward.

Review your plans each morning before you report to work. This should be a tendency.

3. Decide Priorities.

This is the know-how for concentrating on tasks to achieve the greatest results in the shortest amount of time. We are aware that many trained professionals, particularly group leaders, attempt to manage all of this and suffer from a lack of time for many activities. Because nobody has more than 24 hours in a day, concentration is essential for effective time management and productivity.

Eisenhower technique is one of the most mind-blowing time management strategies. It begins with a statement from the 34th President of the United States, Dwight D. Eisenhower: "I have two types of problems: critical and significant. The critical is rarely significant, whereas the significant is seldom dire." Utilize independent sites if you lack an internal coworker to delegate non-essential work.

Chapter 20: Individualized Time Management For All

To summarise, we should investigate questions that will assist you in organising your schedule in the most efficient manner, as self-actualization is the primary objective task.

What personal qualities enable you to accomplish more? Which ones could be enhanced?

How well could you ever organise your day/week/month? Do you require unique programming for alarms or updates, or could you possibly remember everything?

And your fundamental justification? How effectively could you adapt your ongoing activities to broader objectives?

Do you possess sufficient self-control to adapt to work-related issues from a distance (while quarantined globally)? Could you at some point designate specific areas for routine tasks without assistance?

How would you monitor the development, and do you require external oversight?

Define, in light of your responses to the preceding inquiries, which abilities you ought to hone and which assistant devices you could utilise to oversee your time and individual productivity like a pro! ;)

How efficiently do you manage your time? If you are like the majority of people, your response may not be completely certain! Perhaps you feel overburdened and frequently need to burn the midnight oil to meet deadlines. Alternately, your days may appear to alternate between crises, which is distressing and debilitating.

Many of us recognise that we could manage our time more effectively; however, it can be difficult to identify our mistakes and determine how to improve. Nonetheless, when we truly manage our time well, we are particularly effective workers, and our levels of anxiety decrease. We can devote time to high-reward, high-interest projects that can have a real impact on a profession. So, we are happier! The following are ten of the most common time-management mistakes, as well as the systems and strategies you can use to avoid them.

1. Failing to Maintain a Daily Plan.

Have you ever had the nagging feeling that you neglected to complete a significant piece of work? If this is the case, you probably do not utilise a daily schedule to maintain order. (Or alternatively, if you do, you will likely not utilise it effectively!)

The trick to effective daily planning is concentrating on the tasks on your schedule. Numerous individuals use the A-to-F coding framework (A for high need things, F for extremely low needs). Alternatively, this can be improved by using A through D or numbers. If you have extensive tasks on your list, unless you are cautious, the passages for these tasks may be unclear and insufficient. For instance, you may be required to write "Begin financial plan proposal" on paper. Nonetheless, what does this entail? The lack of points of interest in this area may cause you to hesitate or miss crucial steps. Ensure that you divide large projects or endeavours into distinct, significant stages, so that you don't overlook anything essential. You can also use Action Programs to manage your work when multiple large projects are occurring simultaneously. (Action Programs are "modernised" adaptations of day-to-day plans.)

Not Having Personal Objectives

Do you have at least a general idea of where you want to be in six months? What will be said about this time next year, or even centuries from now? If not, now is the time to establish some individual goals! Individual objective setting is essential for effective time management, as objectives provide a direction and purpose to pursue. When you know where you need to go, you can manage your needs, time, and resources to get there. In addition, objectives assist you in determining which endeavours merit your time and which are simply distractions.

3. Not Setting Priorities

Your partner has just walked in with an urgent matter that she wants you to handle immediately, but you are occupied generating ideas for another client. You are confident that you are on the verge of conceiving a brilliant idea for their advertising campaign, but you risk losing the thread of your reasoning along these lines: "crisis."

Occasionally, it can be difficult to determine where to direct your attention, especially when you're confronted with an avalanche of seemingly dire tasks. However, in order to better manage your time, it is essential to learn how to focus on tasks effectively. The "Action Priority Matrix" is a tool that can help you focus on what's important by determining whether a project is high-return and high-need, or low-respect, "fill in" work. If you are aware of the distinction, you will manage your time much more effectively throughout the day.

4. Failing to Monitor Interruptions

Do you realise that some of us lose up to two hours per day due to interruptions? Imagine how much you could accomplish if you had that time back! Whether they originate from messages, IM visits, partners in an emergency, or client calls, interruptions prevent us from achieving flow, which is the enjoyable and ostensibly effortless work that we perform when we are fully engaged in a task.

If you want to effectively manage your day and carry out your most important responsibilities, you must know how to limit interruptions and supervise interferences. For instance, turn off your IM chat when you want to concentrate, and let people know if they're constantly distracting you. At the very least, you should learn how to improve your focus when interruptions occur.

5. Delayed Action

Procrastination occurs when you delay activities that you should be focusing on right now. When you procrastinate, you feel regret that you haven't started; you develop a fear of completing the task; and in the end, everything finds you when you fail to complete the work on time. Start by taking our procrastination test to determine if procrastination is a problem in your life. If this is the case, familiarise yourself with the techniques necessary to overcome procrastination.

For instance, one useful technique is to inform yourself that you will begin a task in ten minutes. Frequently, slackers believe that they must complete a task from start to finish, and this expectation causes them to feel overwhelmed and restless. Overall, focus on devoting a small amount of time to the beginning. There is nothing else to say! Additionally, you may find Activity Plans helpful. These aid you in dividing enormous tasks into manageable chunks, making it easier to see what needs to be done and allowing you to complete smaller chunks simultaneously. This will prevent you from feeling overwhelmed at the start of another task.

Taking on an extreme undertaking

True If this is the case, you most likely have an excessive number of activities and responsibilities. This can result in poor performance, stress, and low morale. Or, you may be an overbearing boss: someone who insists on controlling or performing all of the actual work because they cannot trust anyone else to do it accurately. (This is a problem for everyone, not just chiefs!)

In either case, taking on too much is a poor use of your time, and it can result in a reputation for delivering rushed, sloppy work.

7. In full bloom with "Occupied"

Certain individuals derive pleasure from being busy. The barely met time constraints, the extensive messages, the piles of documents requiring attention in the work area, and the mad dash to the meeting... What a rush of adrenaline! The issue is that "dependence on activity" rarely indicates strength, and it can result in stress. Overall, you should attempt to dial back and learn how to better manage your time.

8. completing a variety of tasks

To stay on top of her responsibilities, Linda routinely composes emails while speaking with clients on the phone. Despite the fact that Linda believes that this is a good use of her time, it can take 20 to 40 percent more time to complete a list of tasks when you perform multiple tasks, as opposed to completing the same list of tasks sequentially. Her messages are riddled with errors, and her customers are confused by her lack of concentration. Thus, the best course of action is to disregard performing multiple tasks and, instead, concentrate on each task individually. Thus, you will produce more excellent work.

9. Not Enjoying Reprieves.

It is ideal to believe that you can work for 8 to 10 hours consecutively, especially when working under a deadline. However, it is beyond the realm of possibility for anyone to concentrate and produce exceptionally high-quality work without resting and recharging their brains. Therefore, do not justify breaks as "with nothing to do." They provide significant free time, which enables you to think creatively and work effectively.

If you find it difficult to stop working, schedule breaks or set a warning as an update. Take a quick walk, grab a cup of coffee, or simply sit and reflect at your desk. Attempt to take some time off every so often. In addition, be sure to give yourself sufficient time for lunch; if you're rushed, you won't produce quality work!

10. inadequately planning activities

Could it be said that you are a morning person? Alternately, do you experience a decline in energy as the sun sets? We all have different circadian rhythms, or at least distinct times of day when we feel generally productive and vivacious.

You can maximise your time by scheduling high-regard tasks during your rush hour and low-energy tasks (such as phone calls and email browsing) during your "down time." Our article, Is This a Morning Job?, explains how to accomplish this. When you create an opportunity to eliminate these errors, it will have a significant impact on your productivity, as well as make you happier and reduce your stress levels.

Chapter 21: Advantages Of Time Management

Time management is the process of organising and planning how to allocate time to specific tasks and objectives. Time management can help you form better habits and be more productive, as well as improve your concentration, boost your confidence, and allow you to better plan your time.

Good time management allows leaders, entrepreneurs, and small business owners to achieve their objectives. When you effectively manage your time, your work-life balance and happiness will improve. Good time management also reduces stress and facilitates goal attainment.

Time management will benefit you in all aspects of life. Time management is crucial for establishing better priorities and increasing productivity.

The better you manage your time, the more effectively you can work smarter, not harder, allowing you to accomplish more in less time and seize more opportunities. Time management is essential for maximising your abilities and organising your day effectively. Good time management allows you to work smarter rather than harder, resulting in the completion of more productive work in less time. I will discuss the advantages of time management and offer suggestions for improving your time management skills.

The advantages of time management are evident. Effective time management allows you to accomplish more with much less effort. This means you have more time to focus on other tasks and can be more productive as a result. Additionally, you spend more time with the people who are most important to you.

In addition, they reduce procrastination and distractions. By taking charge of your time, you can improve your time management skills. It also makes it easier for you to perform essential tasks, such as visiting the doctor.

Time management prevents you from becoming overwhelmed and ensures that you are not always exhausted. The more effectively you manage your time, the more productive you can be with it. Productivity allows you to stay on top of your to-do list and prioritise the most essential tasks. The manner in which you spend your time is now more transparent, and you need not worry about it.

Reducing stress increases productivity, improves sleep quality, and contributes to a healthier work-life balance. Make a move. Determine three stressors that influence your time management skills. Determine the sources of your stress and the impact that eliminating them would have on your life. Select the most significant source of stress and develop a plan to reduce it. The sensation of being overwhelmed is a common source of stress.

Time management can help you achieve a better work-life balance, which is one of the most crucial factors. To be more productive at work and spend more time with the most important people in your life. Work-life balance ensures that your professional and personal lives are harmonious. If you work too many hours, you may experience constant fatigue.

Utilize time-management skills so that you can spend more time on the things that matter most in your life. A good time manager ensures that your time is spent on the most essential tasks. When you organise your affairs, you will have more time to do something you enjoy.

Consider what you could accomplish with an additional five to ten hours per week. Consider the impact that doing the three most important things would have on your life if you accomplished them. Then, to make these changes a reality, develop a detailed action plan.

Time management is crucial for improving concentration and prioritisation. Time management is the most effective method for enhancing concentration and taking charge of your day. Effective time management does not necessitate adding additional tasks or working longer hours. When managing time, it is necessary to work smarter, not harder. This facilitates the formation of good habits. It also ensures that you devote more time to activities that help you achieve your objectives.

When you master time management, you can work faster and accomplish more. Skills in time management can help reduce stress and maximise your time. Effective time management allows you to determine what you wish to accomplish and which tasks are most essential. To make things even better, you'll have more time to pursue goals that are larger and more ambitious.

When you do not effectively manage your time, you procrastinate. It is very easy to put things off until the last minute if your goals aren't clear and focused.

Time management enables you to avoid procrastination because you feel in control of your work. If you feel organised and in control of your time, you are less likely to procrastinate. Create a list of the three primary causes of your procrastination and the first step you can take to address each one.

One of the most significant advantages of time management is increased energy and motivation. Working longer and harder could result in constant fatigue, resulting in constant fatigue. If you have effective time management skills, you will have greater energy and productivity control. Energy is one of the primary benefits of time management.

Maintaining a high level of energy will assist you in time management and increase your productivity. Make a note each time you experience fatigue and lack of energy throughout the week.

There are methods for effective time management that allow for more time to think and plan. Planning your schedule enables you to devote more time to the most important activities. You will have more time to plan, giving you more time to achieve your objectives. Make a move. At the end of each day, jot down three things that make you happy and three things that frustrate you.

www.ingramcontent.com/pod-product-compliance
Lightning Source LLC
Chambersburg PA
CBHW050243120526
44590CB00016B/2201